HOW TO SNEAK MORE MEDITATION INTO YOUR LIFE

K. Kris Loomis

How to Sneak More Meditation Into Your Life: A
Doable Meditation Plan for Busy People

K. Kris Loomis

ISBN: 9781520511115
ASIN: B01FSXA1WA

Dedication

For my yoga students, past and present.

CONTENTS

Author's Note 3
Introduction 3
How to Use This Book 6

Chapter 1 What is Meditation? 9
What is Meditation? 10
Two Main Types of Meditation 11
Common Misconceptions 13

Chapter 2 Focused Attention, or Concentration 18
Introduction to the Focused Attention Meditations 19
The Breathing Meditation 21
Breath Awareness 22
The Sight Meditations 24
Actual Object (Sight) 25
Imagined Object (Sight) 27
Candle Gazing 28
The Sound Meditations 30
External Sound 31
Produced Sound 32
The Touch Meditations 34
Actual Object (Touch) 35

Imagined Object (Touch) 36
The Eating Meditations 38
Taste 39
Tracing Origin 40
The Contemplation Meditations 43
Quotes 44
Affirmations 45
The Drawing Meditations 47
Repetitive Drawing 49
Free Drawing 51
The Walking Meditations 53
Attention Walking 54
Counting Steps 55

Chapter 3 Open Monitoring, or Mindfulness 57
Introduction to the Open Monitoring Meditations 58
External Mindfulness 60
Internal Mindfulness 62

Conclusion 64
About the Author 66
One Last Thing 66

AUTHOR'S NOTE

I would like to thank my beta readers, Hugh Loomis (my most ardent supporter and fan) and Angela Hardin (my buyer of chairs). This book would not have been possible without your valuable feedback!

INTRODUCTION

Shortly after I finished writing my first book, *How to Sneak More Yoga Into Your Life: A Doable Yoga Plan for Busy People*, I gave a workshop on meditation. After the workshop was over, I realized that, like yoga, meditation is something that people know is good for them, but have no idea how to go about starting a practice. Unfortunately, there is a lot of confusion about what meditation is, so I set out with this book to demystify this ancient practice and demonstrate how easy it is to "sneak" meditation into your life, too!

My goal in this book is to introduce you to simple meditation techniques so that you can easily practice them for real-life benefits, such as reduced stress and anxiety, improved sleep, and a better ability to learn new material. Meditating on a regular basis can also prevent you from multi-tasking too often and can help foster creativity and mental focus. Meditating can help lower blood pressure and it also gives your immune system a boost. People who meditate regularly often report an overall feeling of peace and well-being that lasts long after their meditation session ends. So with all of these benefits, why aren't more people meditating?

I have heard many excuses from people about why they "can't" meditate. The two most common excuses are 1) I'm too busy and don't have the time, and 2) I can't sit still. In this book, I will address these excuses, as well as others, such as, I don't know how to do it, it hurts to sit like a pretzel, I think it's boring, and I just can't shut my mind off.

The whole premise of my first book, *How to Sneak More Yoga Into Your Life*, is that we should utilize the times in our lives that I like to call "empty zones." These are times when you are waiting for something or someone, or are kind of stuck between tasks. Why not use that free time for something productive, like yoga or meditation? After all, one minute of yoga or meditation is better than no minutes of yoga or meditation!

If you have ever been curious about meditation, or have tried meditation in the past and just didn't "get" it, then this book is for you. There are as many different types of meditations as there are learning styles, so I am confident that you will find something here that will work for you. Let's get started!

HOW TO USE THIS BOOK

As you work through this book, keep in mind that not every exercise will resonate with you. However, I encourage you to try each style, because it will allow you to objectively assess what works for you and what doesn't.

For example, I have never considered myself a "visual" learner. When I started meditating, I just assumed that any meditation that required visualization would be difficult for me, so I shied away from that type. But after years of experimenting, I have learned that I don't really have problems with visualization after all. As a matter of fact, meditations that involve visualization are now some of my favorites. Don't assume you can't do something, because you might just surprise yourself!

I suggest that you spend two to three days with each technique. By the end of the book, you will feel drawn to what will work for you, both timewise and comfort-wise. It is common for a person to practice one technique for several months or years, and then switch to a different method. I have also known people that do a different meditation each day. There is no right or wrong. After experimenting with the different styles presented in this book you will have a better understanding of what might work for you now. But know that at some point down the road you may want to change approaches and try something new.

Make a commitment to yourself today to do something good for your mental well-being. Many of us find time to go to the gym, or run, or practice yoga because we know that these things are good for us. Unfortunately, we totally neglect one of our most important assets, our brain. For optimal health, our brains need to be worked just as much as our bodies do. What good is having a "buff" body if we have a mushy brain?

Set out to identify the "empty zones" in your life, then use that free time to your advantage. Meditation does not have to take a big chunk of time to be effective. But no one else can meditate for you, so you will have to be willing to experiment and do the work to reap the benefits. Meditation is the workout your brain has been waiting for!

K. Kris Loomis

CHAPTER ONE
What is Meditation?

What is Meditation?

So what is meditation? When I ask this question I usually get an interesting array of answers. "It's sitting still and zoning out," is a common response, and "it means to clear your mind" is another. People also tend to think of meditation as some bizarre New Age nonsense or something that will conflict with their religious, or non-religious, views. Some people think it is nothing more than relaxation. In today's world, who has time to "zone out" or sit around doing nothing?

Meditation is actually a *conscious* focusing on something, either external or internal. What you use as the object of your focus is not terribly important. What is important is that you try to pay attention to that object to the exclusion of everything else. It could be your breath, a word, a sound, or a thought. It could be a picture or your sleeping baby. You could meditate on a favorite quote, or on a hot air balloon floating by. Anything, technically, could serve as your point of focus.

Think of meditation as a mental exercise. If you have ever worked out with weights, you know that you gradually increase your reps with practice. The same goes for meditation. With practice, you gradually increase your ability to concentrate, honing in on your point of focus with fewer distractions.

One of the things I love about meditation is that you can practice it anywhere. And it doesn't take as much time as people think. In fact, sometimes you can use what you are currently doing as your point of focus, which helps eliminate all the multi-tasking and time juggling we have fallen prey to.

There are two main types of meditation, Focused Attention, and Open Monitoring. Go on to the next section to learn the difference between these two types of meditation.

Two Main Types of Meditation

The two main types of meditation are Focused Attention, also referred to as Concentration, and Open Monitoring, often called Mindfulness. Both are legitimate approaches, and you will need to experiment with both to understand which one might work best for you starting out.

Focused Attention, or Concentration, means that you focus your awareness and attention toward one thing only. You consciously pick something to look at, listen to, or think about exclusively for the amount of time you have chosen to practice. Your only job is to stay focused on that one object. If this sounds scary, don't worry. I will be giving you tips along the way to ensure that you have a good practice session, even on the days when you are battling a monkey mind.

Open Monitoring, or Mindfulness, means that you become aware of your entire field of attention in a nonjudgmental way. This is like watching a movie. When you are watching a movie, you don't have any control over what's happening up on the screen, and you often don't have any idea what's coming next. During Open Monitoring meditation you don't try to change or control anything. Rather, you become a bystander and observe things happening around you. This observation without intervention helps develop detachment, which is a really good thing if you tend to cling to drama in your life.

As with all worthwhile things in life, one must stop *thinking* about doing that thing, and just start *doing* it. So I encourage you to stop thinking about practicing meditation and begin, in earnest, practicing it. I am sure that by the time you work your way through this book, you will have found a couple of techniques that you can "sneak" into your life on a consistent basis. Your mind will be forever grateful!

Common Misconceptions

I would like to take a little time to address some common misconceptions that people have about meditation. We, humans, tend to form preconceived ideas about things, and our thoughts about meditation are no exception. Here are some things I have heard others say about meditation over the years:

1. I have to sit cross-legged or in that painful lotus position.

As long as you are keeping your spine straight, you can sit any way you like. You can even sit in a chair if it is difficult for you to get down on the floor. There is no reason to be uncomfortable while meditating. I have known people that practice meditation while lying down, but I don't suggest that for beginners because it's too easy to get sleepy!

2. I have to be still to meditate.

As you work through the book, you will see that there are several exercises that involve movement. Some people are really drawn to these movement oriented meditations, while others prefer quieter meditations. Please experiment with both kinds so that you can find what works best for YOU.

3. I have to close my eyes.

There are plenty of meditations that require visual attention on a certain object with open eyes.

4. I have to wear special clothes.

As long as what you are wearing is comfortable, you are good to go!

5. Meditation takes too much time.

A successful meditation can be as short as one conscious breath. Most people will increase the amount of time they practice over time, but even if you only have one spare minute you can have a successful meditation.

6. I need everything to be quiet in order to meditate.

I put off meditation for years because I could never find a way to turn off all the noise around me. Cars would drive by, the refrigerator would hum, the clock would tick, the neighbor's dog would start barking, it went on and on. Those are EXCUSES. One of my best meditation sessions happened at a busy bus stop. And you will find out that focusing on sound is one of the easiest ways to "sneak" meditation into your life.

7. Meditation is too hard.

People tend to think this because we are a goal-oriented society obsessed with end results. Meditation is a **PROCESS** that may or may not yield the results you expect. Don't worry about the results, because they change over time anyway. Just put in the effort, and everything else will fall into place. Meditation is one of the easiest things you can do because it is foolproof. Really!

8. Meditation is boring.

Meditation tends to awaken the natural curiosity we lose as we grow into adulthood and amass real world problems. When we are curious about something there is little room for boredom because our minds are occupied.

9. I can't shut my mind off.

You don't have to! There are many meditation

techniques that involve following random thoughts as fast as they appear. An active mind can be a great point of focus, as long as the focus is done as an observer to the thoughts with no intervention or manipulation.

10. I don't know how to meditate.

Isn't that why you bought this book? I have been in your shoes, and I know how difficult it is to get started. That's why I want to share with you how easy it is to "sneak" this wonderful practice into your life.

CHAPTER TWO
Focused Attention, or Concentration

Introduction to the Focused Attention Meditations

The Focused Attention approach to meditation means that you will only have one specific point of focus. This point of focus could be anything, really, as long as you throw ALL of your attention to that one thing. Remember that this is simply a way to train your brain. Nothing about this is esoteric.

In this section, I will present several exercises that mostly revolve around the senses. The senses are a great vehicle to use as a point of focus and meditation because many exercises based on the senses are easy to "sneak" in while going about your daily business. Others you will want to set aside a little time for, but often times you can use your "empty zones," or times you are stuck waiting. When you tap into your "empty zones" you are really not having to come up with "extra" time in your day.

If you only take one thing away from this book, let it be this. If you become distracted while you are meditating, all you have to do is acknowledge the distraction, then gently redirect your attention to your object of focus. That's it! If you become distracted 100 times during your meditation, as long as you redirect your attention 101 times, you can count the session a success. You cannot fail!

The Breathing Meditation

I wanted to present the Breath Awareness exercise first because I believe it is the easiest one to sneak into your life. It is a no-brainer. EVERYBODY can do this one because we always have our breath with us. And it can be practiced ANYWHERE. At work, at school, in the shower, before a meeting, in line at the bank, in bed before you drift off, at your kid's baseball game…literally anywhere. You really have no excuse not to "sneak" this one in.

Breath Awareness

All that is required to practice this exercise is that you pay attention to your breath. That's it. You will be successful if you observe one breath or two hundred breaths, so this one is super easy to "sneak" in.

Remember what I said about meditation awakening our natural curiosity? Use that to your advantage in this, and the following exercises.

Ask yourself what part of your body moves the most when you breathe. Does your breath go all the way down to your abdomen, or does it seem to get stuck in your neck or chest? Is the length of your inhale and exhale the same? If not, which is longer? Can you feel your breath in your back? Do you clench your teeth as you breathe? What is the temperature of the air as it brushes past the back of your throat? Is the temperature of the air the same on the way out? Become very curious about your breath!

TIP:

If you become distracted, simply acknowledge the distraction, then guide your awareness back to your breathing. It may go something like this:

OK, I'm going to practice this breathing thing now. All right. I can feel my breath enter my nose. I can feel it in my chest and upper back. Darn, I forgot to call Sherry about that meeting. Yes, I know I need to call her, so I will call her when I am finished. Right now I am paying attention to my breath. It feels cool on the back of my throat, and I can now feel it in my belly…

Don't dwell on the distractions, simply acknowledge them, tell yourself you will have time to deal with them later, then get back to your exercise. You will be amazed at how quickly you learn to do this. As long as you assure your mind that you are not blowing it off and you really will address the issue later, it will let you get back to what you are doing, which is meditating!

The Sight Meditations

Sight is one of the senses we rely on the most, yet we tend to take our sight for granted. Using sight as part of your meditation practice will feel very natural, and with your curiosity engaged you will begin to interpret your surroundings in a different way. I have included three visual meditations, the Actual Object meditation, the Imagined Object meditation, and Candle Gazing.

Actual Object (Sight)

To begin the Actual Object meditation you need to pick an object you can easily see. It does not have to have any particular meaning to you. It could be a paper clip on your desk, a chair across the room, or your sleeping pet. Don't make this too complicated. Just pick and object and start the exercise.

Allow your curiosity to lead you into the meditation. Let's say I choose the paperclip on my desk. What color is it? Is it a lone paper clip or is it among others? Has it been used before? Does it have its original shape or has it been stretched out from use? Does the light catch it, making it shiny, or is the shadow of my computer making it look dull? Where was that paperclip made? Where was it bought? Who bought it? Am I the first person to use that paperclip? Where will that paperclip end up?

There are a million questions you could ask yourself about a paperclip. The point is, you are training your mind to focus on one thing, even if it is just a mundane office supply. And do you see how this type of meditation can be practiced anywhere? You really don't have to sit cross-legged on a zafu with incense wafting around to have a successful meditation session!

Imagined Object (Sight)

The Imagined Object exercise is the first meditation I present where you will want to close your eyes. This exercise is very much like the previous one, except instead of focusing on an actual object, you will imagine an object in your mind as specifically as you can.

Let's say you want to imagine a box for your meditation session. With your eyes closed, try to conjure up an image of a box. It could be a cardboard box, a jack-in-the-box box, a crate type box, a shoe box, your choice. How much space does that box take up in your mind? What color is it? Does it have anything inside? You know a box has six sides, but how many sides can you actually see in your mind? Are the sides of the box rough or smooth? Does the box have a light shining on it creating a shadow? Is the box on the floor or on the ground? Perhaps suspended by a rope?

TIP:

On the meditations that require you close your

eyes, it is helpful to set a timer on your phone or computer to alert you when your allotted time is up. That way you don't have to keep opening your eyes to check how much time you have left. During your first meditation practices, I suggest that you set the timer for no more than two minutes. As you become more accustomed to the process, you can increase your time gradually.

And remember, if your mind wanders or becomes distracted, simply acknowledge the distraction, then redirect your attention to the object of your meditation.

Candle Gazing

This exercise combines the Actual Object method with the Imagined Object method.

Begin by lighting a candle. Make sure it is in a secure holder and on a flat surface. Sit or stand at least five feet away from the flame.

Now observe the flame. Watch it dance and flicker. Is it the same color throughout, or are there subtle differences in hue? Does the flame stay at the same height, or does it sometimes flatten out? Does it look hot or cool? What is the character or mood of the flame? Does it seem happy, capricious, or ominous?

After several minutes of looking at the flame, close your eyes and try to "see" the flame in your mind. Some people can do this right away, while others may never see the flame with their eyes closed. All you have to do is try. It's the trying that is important, not whether or not you actually see the flame with your eyes closed.

If you have trouble "seeing" the flame in your mind, simply open your eyes and look at the candle some more. You can always try to conjure up the image after more practice.

The Sound Meditations

We are surrounded by sound everywhere we go. At home, the refrigerator hums, the washing machine whirls, the kids squeal and the pets trounce through the house. Perhaps your spouse leaves the radio on in the bathroom every morning. Then there are traffic sounds and announcements on public transit, grocery carts have lopsided wheels and airplanes flying overhead are a fact of life. Even when we go out into the woods for some peace and quiet we cannot silence the sounds of nature. We simply cannot escape the sound of living.

Now many people would say that the sounds of nature are more pleasant than the sounds of everyday life, and there may be some truth to that. But for our purposes, it doesn't really matter what sound you use as your focus. You can choose an External Sound or a Produced Sound.

External Sound

When you are choosing an external sound to be the focus of your attention, make sure that it is a sound that will occur more that a couple of times during your session. If you live in New York City or any big metropolitan area, you could easily pick the sound of a car horn as your focus. But if you live in a small town you may need to pick something a little more appropriate to your area, such as the sound of the guy in the next cubicle typing or the hum of your freezer.

Once you have identified your chosen sound, all you have to do is listen to it. Does it occur regularly? Is it always the same pitch? Does it stay the same volume, or does it fluctuate? Does the sound seem pleasant, angry, or funny? Does it speed up or slow down?

If you become distracted by a different sound, simply acknowledge the distraction, then redirect your attention back to the original sound you chose.

TIP:

It is helpful to decide ahead of time how long your meditation session is going to last. That way, the decision is made and you don't have to think about it anymore. This eliminates uncertainty in your practice. Commit to the time you chose, whether that be one minute or twenty, and keep returning your attention to your chosen object of focus.

Produced Sound

Produced sound is a sound that you make yourself. One of the most common produced sounds in meditation is a mantra, but that may seem weird or foreign to some people. You could produce a sound by striking your pencil against the edge of your desk or by snapping your fingers. Remember, it doesn't have to be complicated!

Once you begin producing your sound, start comparing one repetition to the next. We assume the sound will be exactly the same each time we produce it, but is that really true? Does your produced sound always last the same amount of time? Is it always the same volume? Do you always use the same amount of force to produce the sound? Does your sound seem plump, or stringy? Is it melodious or percussive? Is it a pleasant sound? Perhaps mechanical in nature?

If you are working with a mantra, how does the produced sound feel in your throat? In your chest? Can you feel the vibrations in your body? How does producing the sound affect your breathing?

The Touch Meditations

Touch is another of the sense awareness meditations that is easy to "sneak" into your life. This is something that people don't often think about including when they discuss meditation, but touch can be a powerful way to improve your ability to focus.

Human touch is valuable, and most people function better when they have regular contact with another living being. Unfortunately, we don't consciously process the sensation while it is happening. Using touch as a focus of meditation will allow you to appreciate the touch you experience in your daily life on a whole new level.

When exploring the touch meditations you can choose between an actual object, or an imagined one, just as you did in the section on sight meditation.

Actual Object (Touch)

You have many choices when it comes to picking a touch focus. You could hold your daughter's teddy bear, a cereal bowl, your favorite pen, a paperback novel, your husband's watch, or the TV remote. And it is perfectly OK to choose an object that you just touch rather than hold. It would be difficult to hold your car. Use your imagination!

Because this meditation is about the sense of touch, you want to focus on what your object FEELS like. Does it feel smooth or rough? Hot or cold? Furry or spiky? Does it feel deep or shallow? If your object has edges, do they feel sharp or rounded? Does this object feel sturdy? Flimsy?

Really get curious about this object. And just because it may be something you see or use every day don't assume that you know everything there is to know about it. Pretend that you don't know *anything* about this object and the only way you can learn about it is through your sense of touch. You might just learn something new about your TV remote!

TIP:

For maximum benefit, do this meditation exercise with your eyes closed if possible. We tend to give ourselves over to sight, so if you close your eyes you will have to "see" the object a new way.

Imagined Object (Touch)

This Imagined Object exercise is very much like the Imagined Object for sight exercise earlier in the book. The only difference is that you want to focus on the imagined *feel* of the object, not what the object looks like.

I like to imagine what it would feel like to wear certain clothes. How would the fabric feel against my skin? How would a satin dress feel as opposed to a burlap sack? How would the weight of the fabric feel against my thighs as opposed to my shins? Would it feel heavy or light? Would it feel restrictive or airy?

Of course, you could choose something that you could hold in your imagination instead of wear.

It's always your choice!

TIP:

Try not to get frustrated if the imagined exercises are initially more difficult for you, because you can ultimately choose to practice another style of meditation. There are many other meditations left in the book to try, and these are just the tip of the iceberg, so don't despair!

The Eating Meditations

Because we are always in such a hurry we rarely slow down long enough to enjoy our food. We don't appreciate how it tastes or where it came from. We tend to take these things for granted.

In my own practice, I have found that consciously meditating on the food I eat has given me a greater understanding of how the food business works, and how I feel about that. I tend to make smarter choices in my diet. I eat more slowly and enjoy my food more. And I really appreciate it now when my husband cooks a complicated dish!

The two eating meditations I have included in this book are the Taste meditation and the Tracing Origin meditation. Because we tend to, more or less, eat three meals a day (plus snacks), you will have many opportunities to "sneak" these two meditations in.

Taste

The Taste meditation simply revolves around the sensory aspect of eating. You can do this meditation on one type of food only, or you could vary the object of focus to include everything on your plate.

I like to begin this meditation by visually assessing my food. What colors are represented on my plate? What am I expecting the food to taste like before I place a bite in my mouth? Taste is connected to smell, so this is a great way to get your olfactory sense involved as well. After your food has passed through the visual and olfactory senses, compare the actual taste to any preconceived notions. Does your food taste like what it looks and smells like?

If you are focused on one food only, try putting it on different parts of your tongue to see if it changes the taste. Also, ask yourself if the taste is consistent bite to bite. Not only do you want to taste the food, you want to notice the texture of the food as well. Is it creamy or crunchy? Spongy? Is it cold, hot, or room temperature? Does it squish between your teeth, or get caught between your teeth?

Eating ice cream and eating popcorn are two very different experiences!

TIP:

Keep in mind that meditation is a skill-based practice. So the more you practice, the better your skills of observation will become. So it really doesn't matter if you only "meditate" on one or two bites. If you practice, you will improve your skills, and eventually be able to focus on your food for an entire meal.

Tracing Origin

The Tracing Origin meditation is one of my favorites. I find if fascinating to think about and practice.

This meditation begins by picking a food focus. You pick a food item on your plate, then trace its origin as far back as you can imagine. What journey did that food item take to get to your plate? How many people touched that item from its inception to the table? Now it is true that we can't know *exactly* how those french fries landed there, but just thinking about it can be eye-opening, to say the least.

Let's start with a simple carrot. For example, I see steamed carrots on my plate. I start thinking backward. Who cut the carrots up before they were cooked? Were they taken out of a bag? Where did that bag come from, the grocery store? Who put the bag of carrots on the shelf? Who unpacked the box of bagged carrots? Who took the carrots off the truck? How far did the truck have to travel to get the carrots to the store? Where was the bag of carrots packed? Did a person pack the bag, or was it a machine? Did the carrots grow on a farm out in the open air exposed to the elements, or in a controlled environment? Who or what picked the carrot? How long did it take the carrot to grow from seed? A question I like to ask myself is how many people did it take to get that carrot to my table?

Now imagine that you are eating a steak. You begin asking yourself how that steak got to your table. It becomes a little more complicated, doesn't it? You have to imagine not only how that steak got there, but the entire life of the animal and who took care of it, what it ate, how it was butchered, and so on. This is not meant to gross anyone out, or to try and turn everyone into vegetarians. I am only saying that once you go through this exercise you have a greater respect for how much effort, time, and expense it takes to have dinner. I now have a much greater appreciation for farmers and the thankless job they do for the greater populace.

Now if you really want to have fun with this, trace the origin of the next candy bar you eat. Look at the ingredients and imagine where they all came from. How does one partially hydrogenate soybean oil, anyway? Who does that? And if they only use egg whites, what happens to all those yolks? I have had to, on occasion, look up a word from the ingredients list, and STILL had no idea how to trace its origin. Funny, but I don't eat many candy bars anymore.

TIP:

Once you have done the Tracing Origin exercise with food several times, you will find yourself being more curious about where other things in your life come from and what had to happen to bring them into your life. You can use this meditation on ANYTHING, which is why it is such a great one to "sneak" in.

The Contemplation Meditations

We have all heard the expression, "Let me meditate on that." Indeed, contemplation is a form of meditation because it is thoughtful and focused attention on a saying, quote, or situation.

Just as with the other exercises in the book, you can pick any thought to meditate on. What you choose to contemplate doesn't have to be anything special or magical. However, I believe if you are going to take the time to think about a quote or affirmation, it might as well be an uplifting one!

Quotes

The quote you choose to meditate on could be from a book you are reading or an inspirational quote from a historical figure. It could be a bible verse. It could even be a snippet of conversation you overheard while waiting for your coffee at the neighborhood cafe. I tend to pick quotes from the great thinkers because it is interesting to me to think about something someone said so long ago that might still have meaning in today's society.

I like quotes from Seneca and Socrates. Seneca advises, "After you have run over many thoughts, select one to be thoroughly digested that day." I will often pick a passage from a book I am currently reading to meditate on. Some will find curiosity about a song lyric.

You can begin by asking yourself what the quote means to you on the surface. How could this impact your life? Your significant other's life? The lives of your friends? Does it have any value on a societal level? A global level?

There is really no right or wrong way to do this. And it is possible that your thoughts on the quote may change over time. Sometimes I find that the quote I have chosen to think about one day stays with me for awhile. Just remember that for the allotted time you have chosen to "meditate" on your quote, redirect your attention back to it if your mind wanders off and begins thinking about something else.

Affirmations

Affirmations are statements that are meant to improve our emotional state. They tend to be short statements that we think or say out loud. They are meant to inspire, strengthen, and encourage.

Some common affirmations are: I trust myself, I replace my anger with understanding and compassion, I release the false stories I make up in my head, I forgive myself, This day brings me joy, I let go of worries that drain my energy, I will follow my dreams, and so on. You can look for affirmations on the internet, or you can write your own.

When you use an affirmation as part of a meditation session, pick how long you want to meditate, then repeat your affirmation, either out loud or in your head, like a mantra, until your time runs out. You may even find your affirmation coming to you at other times during your day. If so, great! It only means that you are focusing on positive possibilities that you would like to become your reality.

I have known people who have used affirmations to help them get over a bad relationship, to lose weight, to quit smoking, and to finish a college degree, so don't hesitate to experiment with this type of meditation.

The Drawing Meditations

If you have been having a difficult time so far, this drawing meditation may be the one for you! It is the first meditation in the book that requires you to take physical action. If you love to doodle or draw, then why not use that as a focus of meditation?

I present two types of drawing meditation, although there are others. The nice thing about a drawing meditation is that all you need is a writing instrument and a piece of paper, or a drawing app on your phone, tablet, or computer. This is different, however, from regular drawing. When we think of drawing we are generally concerned with an end result. If you use drawing as a meditation, you are more concerned with the PROCESS of drawing and using your power of observation during that process.

You can meditate using Repetitive Drawing, or

you can let your imagination reign with Free Drawing.

Repetitive Drawing

Repetitive Drawing requires that you pick something to draw that is easy to replicate or repeat. It could be a symbol, a letter, a number, or even a word. You have a lot of freedom with these drawing meditations, so use your imagination and be creative.

Once you have chosen something to draw, you simply begin drawing that symbol over and over on the same page. You could start at the top left-hand corner and draw line by line as if you were writing a letter, or you could jump around the page drawing your symbol. You could even draw a bigger symbol with a lot of little ones.

As you continue drawing, notice the pressure it takes to make your image. Is each image you produce the same size each time? If you are using a pencil, does the line get thicker as your point wears down? If you are using a pen, does the ink flow freely, or are there hiccups in the ink flow? What does the writing utensil feel like in your hand? If you are drawing with your finger on a screen, what is the temperature of the screen? If you are drawing a line, is the line straight, or does it rise or fall toward the end of the page? Be very curious about the marks you are making.

Try not to draw on autopilot. Really immerse yourself in the repetitive action. If you find your mind wandering during your drawing session, acknowledge it, then simply start asking yourself questions about the quality of your images.

Free Drawing

Free Drawing is just what it sounds like. Some people would call this doodling, but others see it as a greater means of expression. You put the pen or pencil to paper and let your subconscious guide you.

You may want to set a certain amount of time aside for the actual meditative drawing and use another block of time to interpret your drawing. Honestly, that last step is optional, although some people really enjoy trying to make sense of their drawings at a later time.

Remember this is the process of immersing yourself in the DOING of drawing. How the pencil feels in your hand. The sound the pen makes as it glides across the page. Noticing the lights and shadows that fall across your work. You may even want to use color.

TIP:

Sometimes these drawing meditations evoke

emotion. You may feel inspired as you draw, or sad, or angry. Don't judge the feeling, rather notice it as if you were observing it in someone else.

This is a type of meditation that you will probably want to set a timer for. It is amazing how "lost" you can become in the process. It can be a very fun way to meditate!

The Walking Meditations

Walking makes a great meditation! Even though most of us don't walk as much as we should, any type of walking will serve for meditation purposes. Walking around the mall, walking from the parking lot to the grocery store, walking from the laundry room to the bedroom to put up your clothes, walking up steps, walking on the beach, anywhere you walk you can use that time as meditation time.

As with the other meditations I have outlined in this book, there are many ways to do a walking meditation. I have included two walking meditations here for you to experiment with, Attention Walking and Counting Steps.

Attention Walking

Attention Walking is a type of meditation that allows you to become consciously aware of the sensation of walking in real time. A word of caution. You do not want to do this in a high traffic area. Use common sense when you do this meditation and always make sure you are in a safe environment.

After about three years old, we take the actions associated with walking for granted. We don't have to try and walk, we just do it. For walking to become a meditation you need to deconstruct the actions that have to occur to transport your body from point A to point B. Ask yourself what goes on mechanically in the body. How does it feel when you shift your weight from one foot to the other? How does that affect your balance? Does your stride feel even, or uneven? What do your feet feel when they touch the ground? Do you walk heel to toe or toe to heel? Do you tend to roll onto the outside of your feet or collapse in toward the arch? How do your knees feel as you walk? Your lower back? If you are walking barefooted, do your toes feel free and open, or tight? If you are wearing shoes, do your feet feel cramped inside the shoes, or are the shoes loose on your feet? Can you feel your socks? What is your head doing? Looking up and ahead to where you are going, or down at your feet? Do your hands hang by your side or are they swinging to the pace of your steps?

This meditation can last as long as you are walking, or you can set aside part of your stroll to "sneak" in your meditation. Again, make sure you are in a safe environment!

Counting Steps

The Counting Steps meditation is one of the easiest ones in the book. You have many options to choose from, and you may want to experiment with different ways to see what works best for you.

You could simply count your steps as you walk, starting with one and counting up to whatever number you have chosen ahead of time. Or, you could start with, say, one hundred and count backward with each step. Or you could count in twos or fives. You might want to change it up each time you use walking as your point of focus.

TIP:

The key to this meditation is deciding ahead of time how you are counting and to what number. Then, if you become distracted, acknowledge the distraction, and start over. Yes, you need to start over with this one! But keep in mind that it is not important if you actually arrive at your final number, just that you return to the counting after the distraction.

ANOTHER TIP:

You can also experiment with this method by using your breath as your focus instead of your steps. Breathe slowly and deeply and count either each complete breath or count to each inhale and exhale. I like to do this if I am having trouble sleeping. I will start at 100, and it goes something like this: Inhale 100, exhale 99, inhale 98, exhale 97, inhale 96, exhale 95, and so on. I usually have to start over several times, and I usually fall asleep before I finish!

CHAPTER THREE
Open Monitoring, or Mindfulness

Introduction to the Open Monitoring Meditations

The Open Monitoring approach to meditation means that you are consciously aware of everything going on around you, either externally or internally. The important thing is that you observe things in a detached way. You are training yourself to be observant without being reactive. Interaction on your part is not required, and frankly, discouraged.

This type of meditation is often referred to as "mindfulness." Once you have been practicing this meditation style for awhile, you may find yourself able to assess situations more quickly because you will have the ability to do so without judgment. You will simply and honestly see what is before you, the "big picture," so to speak.

This practice can be very liberating because over time you will see how little "control" you have over external things. You will begin to give yourself permission to stop micromanaging those around you and, instead, respect the decisions other people make. You will also begin to notice the "little" things that make life so enjoyable!

I will give you only two exercises here. First, we will look at how to be mindful externally, then we will turn our attention to an internal mindfulness approach.

External Mindfulness

External Mindfulness is an Open Monitoring technique that involves observances outside of your personal thoughts and space. Instead of having only one point of focus, you observe everything you possibly can about your environment, often using your senses to guide you through the process.

Because I want you to understand that this can be practiced anywhere, I will use a restaurant as an example.

Let's say that you have just walked into your favorite restaurant, but they are extremely busy and you have to put your name on a waiting list. You sit at the bar and order a drink as you wait for your name to be called. What can you notice about the bartender? Maybe she is wearing a wrinkled shirt or a stained apron. Does she appear relaxed or rushed? Are her hands delicate, or do they look rough? Painted nails? Is her voice soft, or does she have to speak loudly to be heard over the noise? What does it sound like in the bar? Can you make out individual conversations, or is it cacophonous in that space? Can you hear the glasses clink as the barman puts up the clean glasses? Do the glasses sparkle in the light? Can you see the front entrance reflected in the mirror? What is the predominant smell in the bar? Does it smell like fried food? Look at what people around you are eating. Can you see all of the primary colors, red, blue, and yellow? Notice the man in the corner using his laptop. Is he working? Why did he come to a bar to work? Is he expecting a client to meet him there? How does your glass feel in your hand? Is the glass heavy? What does your drink smell like as you bring it up to your lips? Does your drink taste like you were expecting?

See how your mind is allowed to mentally sweep the area? You can almost imagine your mind is in a bubble just floating around the room, noticing everything from above. Also appreciate that you do not have to DO anything in this meditation, except notice things. You are not responsible for anything that happens in that room.

You can easily involve all of the senses in this exercise, so if you feel yourself beginning to get bogged down in one aspect of the scene, or if you find yourself beginning to focus on a personal problem, simply look somewhere different and start the process over again, using your senses as a guide.

This is a great meditation because you can "sneak" it in anytime you find yourself in an "empty zone." With the availability of current technology, it is very easy to be seduced by our devices, which, I believe, is causing us to be more and more alienated from our surroundings and other people. Only time will tell how constantly being "connected" will affect society, but I, for one, do not want to lose the ability to observe the beauty and complexity of life around me.

Internal Mindfulness

Internal Mindfulness is an Open Monitoring technique that focuses on what is happening with you internally. This is very different than meditating on a current problem or situation where your focus is directed only at that one thing. In this meditation, you allow yourself the freedom to explore what naturally and spontaneously comes to mind. You will want to sit quietly, preferably with your eyes closed. When I practice this type of meditation, I always set a timer.

Start by observing a few breaths. Then mentally step aside and see what comes into your mind. Don't try to control your thoughts, and do not judge them. Be detached from your thoughts, as if they were a separate part of you. Be an observer only. Allow thoughts to come and go, as if they were inside a balloon floating by. Do not hold on to the balloon! Let it float on by. You may become aware of ambient sound. Or the temperature of the room. Or a breeze. Allow your mind the freedom to wander without restriction or expectation.

TIP:

Remember that this is not a problem solving exercise. When you are in the middle of the exercise, there are no problems. Only thoughts. And these thoughts are not good or bad, they just are what they are. Allow them to come and go without becoming attached to them or their deeper meaning.

Conclusion

I hope this book has demonstrated to you that, 1) meditation is not difficult, 2) anyone can reap the rewards of meditation, and 3) meditation is really easy to "sneak" into your life!

Remember that meditation is a skill-based practice, with the focus on the word PRACTICE. However, the practice does not have to be difficult or unenjoyable. Please experiment with the different meditations in the book, and if nothing here resonates with you, I encourage you to keep looking! There are many free guided meditations on the internet and there are even apps dedicated to guided meditations, so keep an open mind and explore all possibilities.

Most of all, have fun with your meditations! Allow yourself to be curious, because it is through curiosity that we learn more about ourselves and the world we live in.

If you enjoyed *How to Sneak More Meditation Into Your Life: A Doable Meditation Plan for Busy People* please check out its companion book, *How to Sneak More Yoga Into Your Life: A Doable Yoga Plan for Busy People*!

Thank you for reading my book.

About the Author

K. Kris Loomis has been teaching and learning from her yoga students for almost 20 years. She has studied yoga with David Swenson, Esther Myers, Stephanie Keach, and Sean Corn. Kris is the author of another nonfiction book, *How to Sneak More Yoga Into Your Life: A Doable Yoga Plan for Busy People*, as well as the the fiction series, "Modern Shorts for Busy People." Kris is a classically trained pianist, a determined chess player, an origami enthusiast, and a playwright.

Visit Kris' website at www.kkrisloomis.com and receive a free short story! You can find her on Facebook, Twitter, and Pinterest.

One Last Thing

If you enjoyed *How to Sneak More Meditation Into Your Life: A Doable Meditation Plan for Busy People* and found it useful, I'd be grateful if you'd post a short review on Amazon. Your support and comments really make a difference, especially to indie authors!

I would also appreciate good old fashioned "word of mouth" to your friends, colleagues, or anyone you think would benefit from having a little more meditation in their life.

Thanks again for your support!

Made in the USA
San Bernardino, CA
05 June 2017